# How to Create An
# Economic
# Democracy

## A Revolutionary New Concept of Economics

## By Richard J. Wilson J.D.

Published January 2012

# Table of Contents

## The Problem

*S. C. Justice Louis D. Brandeis    1856 -- 1941*

*"The greatest problem which is before the American people is the problem of reconciling our industrial system with the political democracy in which we live. . .*

*The civilized world today believes that industrial self-government is impossible, that we must adhere to the system we have known as the monarchical system of master and servant, or as more politely called employer and employee.*

*It rests with America to prove that, as we have in the political world shown what self-government can do, we are to pursue the same lines in the industrial world."*

# Preface

*"Power corrupts, and absolute power corrupts absolutely."*
*Lord Acton*

We like to think we live in an era of democracy. But we know we're just fooling ourselves. We know we still live in an era of oligarchy where one percent of the population controls both our economy and our politics. Like much of the civilized world, we've organized our politics as a democracy, and we go through the motions of democracy at every election, but we know we haven't yet achieved government of the people, by the people, and for the people, because we have an economic oligarchy corrupting both our economy and politics.

The oligarchy is created because our society issues *permanent, unlimited* and *hereditable* power in the form of money to be used to govern our economy. And we know from experience in politics that whenever society issues any kind of *permanent, unlimited* and *hereditable* power to govern anything, a few clever people will ultimately accumulate the power by whatever means possible to become a hereditary oligarchy.

And we know full well that in the presence of raw, unlimited and hereditary money power, people lose their humanity. We have so many examples of the finest and most intelligent of people becoming obsessed with money power, and we've seen them lose whatever morality they may have had. Today a civilized society wouldn't think of issuing raw, unlimited and hereditary political power, but we haven't yet adopted that policy to our economy.

And it wouldn't matter if we switched to socialism or communism, for these 'isms" also use the monetary system to govern the economy and issue the *permanent, unlimited,* and *hereditable* power of money. And they, too, ultimately end with an economic oligarchy ruling the economy and politics. *It's vitally important to recognize that it is the monetary system that creates the oligarchy, and not the variations or 'isms" of the monetary system.*

Our experience is clear. Society cannot create democracy by changing only the political system. If we continue to issue money that grants the bearer *permanent, unlimited,* and *hereditable* power to govern our economy, we will still get oligarchy and all the economic and political injustice oligarchy creates. If we want democracy we must decide to eliminate *all* forms of permanent, unlimited and hereditable power in both politics and economics.

Of course, a modern economy needs a medium of exchange to operate. That's beyond argument. But with today's computer technology a medium of exchange doesn't have to give the bearer *permanent, unlimited* and *hereditable* economic power. We could organize an econoscience to design a new medium that grants people only *limited* economic power and put an end to economic oligarchy, just as we created a political science to design a new political system that grants people *limited* political power to end political oligarchy.

The reason we haven't taken steps to change the system and end the economic oligarchy is we, the people, have an addictive love affair with using the raw, unlimited and hereditable power of money. And it's reasonable to assume, if conditions hadn't changed, as self-destructive as it may be, society could go on for another thousands of years issuing raw, unlimited and hereditable money power and remain stuck in oligarchy with all the injustice it creates.

**BUT CONDITIONS ARE NOW** rapidly changing and the change is accelerating. In the last century science began producing robotics, and as these machines grow ever more human like, they are rapidly replacing human beings in the economy. In the not too distant future, if we continue to use the monetary system, robotics will swallow so many jobs that the majority of people in society will find themselves permanently exiled from participating in our economy.

I realize this may sound like the popular story of extraterrestrial beings invading society, but this is not science fiction. This is actual science. The advance of robotics created by people in white coats is unleashing upon society mechanical replacements to do the work in our economy, and, as long as we use the monetary system, because they demand no salary, these mechanical beings could eventually push the majority of us out of work.

And when that critical point is reached the majority of human beings will surely demand a new system of economics that allows everyone to participate in the economy and enjoy the wealth created by both man and machine. And when that happens, to avoid social disaster, society will need to be ready with a well-tested replacement for the monetary system. We may not like the thought, but the advance of robotics is slowly pushing the monetary system into its twilight years.

We can, of course, deny this is happening, or say to ourselves this won't happen in our lifetime, but it will in the case of the younger generation. Science doesn't progress linearly. It progresses exponentially, and, if we're still using the monetary system, sometime in this century people will be competing with machines able to calculate and perform beyond human capability and work for nothing.

But we needn't despair, for, as we'll see in this book, if we are willing to set aside our emotional attachment to money and put our faith in modern science, science can lead us to a totally new system of economics where economic power is *limited* and we live in an economy run of the people, by the people and for the people. We'll see, thanks to science, if we're wise, human beings can still be the masters of their destiny.

In the opening chapter we'll enlarge on this theme, repeating some points for emphasis. Then, following the scientific method introduced by Francis Bacon, and quoting often from his *Novum Organum,* we'll see how Bacon's new method led John Locke to discover how to organize a political system with *limited* political power to end political oligarchy. And, by following the trail blazed by Locke, we'll find that Bacon's new method will lead us to discover a new economic system that could create a new era of democracy in both politics and economics.

*"One method of delivery alone remains to us; which is simply this: we must lead men to the particulars themselves, and their series and order; while men on their side must force themselves for a while to lay their notions by and begin to familiarize themselves with facts."*

Francis Bacon, *Novum Organum (1620)*

# I

## Our Fading Economic System

The monetary system adopted thousands of years ago in the Age of Faith to govern our economy doesn't work well in our Age of Science. It has never proved to be a very efficient system of economic government. After all of its thousands of years of operation, half the nations of the world still remain sunk in abject poverty, and, of the half that achieved some prosperity, a third of the people in those nations struggle daily to survive.

The problem is the monetary system is too complex for most human beings to master. The vast majority of society gets lost in the emotional intricacies and power plays of the monetary system. They can't bring themselves to generate the aberrant behavior necessary to operate in the system. And, of course, clever people who understand the emotional intricacies and are willing to do so quietly pick their bones.

And the monetary system is also an unstable system for, designed in the Age of Faith, people must have faith in money for it to function, and, since faith ebbs and flows, the economy ebbs and flows, in one season growing, and in another withering. Today the world's economy is ebbing because people's faith in money is ebbing, and the outlook for the restoration of faith is so poor that society has fallen into a worldwide depression.

And the monetary economy is always riddled with corruption and injustice. In fact so much of social immorality is linked to money that early Christian writers like Timothy were led to report that "The love of money is the root of *all* evil." Drug lords, murderers, kidnappers, the politically corrupt, and all sorts of antisocial gangs we read about every day can be directly traced to greed for the raw, unlimited and hereditable power of money.

Our schoolmen want us to believe that all of the inefficiency, instability, and injustice in our economy is created by people who either don't know how to cope in a monetary system or who abuse it. Our schoolmen never blame the monetary system, for, having spent a lifetime promoting it, they want us to assume it is the only system available to govern the economy of a sophisticated society and the greatest boon ever invented by mankind.

But this notion of the schoolmen is not based on fact. We've learned from long experience in politics that it is not people that create social inefficiency, instability and injustice. It is the system of behavior that grants people *permanent, unlimited* and *hereditable* power that corrupts humanity and creates the problems. We've learned from experience in politics that, if we reorganize any system of behavior to *limit* power, the inefficiency, instability and injustice is limited.

It's incredible to imagine that our schoolmen in this 21st century Age of Science would be still preaching, like Dr. Pangloss in Voltaire's *Candid,* that economic oligarchy produces "the best of all possible economic worlds." This is because our schoolmen are not scientists. They are scholastics merely repeating what they've been told by scholarly masters. It never occurs to them that the monetary system might be causing the problems.

But, despite all of its systematic problems, the world has loped along for several thousand years using the monetary system. We regularly complain about the problems, but haven't demanded a change of the system.

Society has bought into the logic of the schoolmen to such an extent, that it seems totally unaware that it is the monetary system creating economic problems, and that society has an inalienable right to replace any system of government that creates such problems. Let's pause a moment to remind ourselves of Jefferson's elegant declaration of that inalienable right:

*"We hold these truths to be self evident, that all men are created equal, that they are endowed by their creator with certain unalienable rights, that among these are life, liberty and the pursuit of happiness – that to secure these rights governments are instituted among men, deriving their just powers from the consent of the governed – that whenever any form of government becomes destructive of these ends, it is the right of the people to alter or to abolish it, and to institute new government laying its foundation on such principles and organizing its powers to such form as to them shall seem most likely to effect their safety and happiness."*

The reason society has bought into the logic of our schoolmen, and not effectively demanded change is that society, as Timothy wrote, is in love with money, and physically addicted to using its raw, unlimited and hereditable power. And, like anyone deeply in love and

14

physically addicted, society is in a state of denial, and emotionally blind to the problems, and can't imagine life without the object of their love and addiction. And society is kept in that blind state by the relentless logic of our schoolmen.

Another reason we do nothing is the monetary system for all of its faults works just well enough to allow the majority of people, about 70% of the population in our society, to achieve some level of prosperity. And, since we live in a political democracy ruled by the majority, the majority has found it too much trouble to worry about problems created by the monetary system that don't personally affect the majority. They're prospering, and look down upon those who don't as somehow inferior people.

The poor, on the other hand, those who bear the brunt of the systemic inefficiency, instability and injustice comprise only a third of our population and are a minority, and, in a political democracy, the minority vote doesn't count. So year after year we continue to use the monetary system, indifferently allowing a third of our population to suffer poverty and injustice, silently hoping the poor and unemployed won't get violent.

This indifference of the prosperous majority to the suffering of the minority is what Madison called "The tyranny of the majority," and is one of the serious unresolved shortcomings of democracy. So, despite the fact that the monetary system is inefficient and unstable and invites tyranny, if conditions hadn't changed, we might very well go on forever using the monetary system, ignoring the booms and busts and the heartaches it creates among the minority.

**BUT TODAY THINGS ARE CHANGING.** In the middle of the last century something new appeared that promises to soon make the monetary system untenable even for the majority. Modern science has introduced robotics. At their introduction in the New York World Fair in 1939, robots were touted as a boon to mankind, because they have the potential of saving mankind from a lot of work.

And the sales pitch has proven to be very true. Robots are relentlessly replacing human beings in the workplace. After the initial cost, these machines demand no salary, never make mistakes, and belong to no unions; so, as the science of robotics improves, robots are proving more desirable employees than human beings in ever expanding areas of the economy.

But, unfortunately, we, the people, are not the beneficiaries of the advancing science, for in the monetary system, if we don't work, we don't get paid. And, if we don't get paid, we can't buy anything to eat, or to wear, or to house us. And, with the steady advance of robotics, very soon robots will exile ever more millions from the economy, and there will be fewer and fewer people buying things.

So, not only are robots hurting people, they are slowly damaging the operation of the monetary system for, since robots and the unemployed don't buy goods and services, the market for goods and services shrinks. And, when the market shrinks, production shrinks, and jobs shrink, and so on. It is conceivable robots will exile so many of us that there will be no market for production, no production, and no economy.

So, where before the advent of robots we could lope along using the monetary system with the majority prospering and the poor minority silent, with the advent of robots the poor may soon become the majority and we'll be faced with a political revolution, or the monetary system may collapse for the lack of a market for goods and services. The fact is the modern science of robotics is slowly destroying the monetary system.

**FORTUNATELY, THE EFFECT** of robotics upon the monetary system has been slow. Spread over many generations, its effect on society and the monetary system has been almost imperceptible. We got an early indication that something was brewing in the 19th century when The Luddites smashed machinery that took their jobs and exiled them from the economy. But the movement petered out because technological advances then began to increase jobs, making it appear for a century or more that the advance of science and technology was beneficial to the monetary system.

The steam engine caused mills to blossom that required so many new workers that even children were employed. The steamboat created jobs in shipbuilding, crewing and dock handling. Railroads expanded the work force so much that America had to import Chinese workers. The telegraph and telephone, radio and TV created a whole new entertainment industry. And Henry Ford's low cost autos triggered the greatest job increase in history.

But then problems began to appear for Henry Ford not only introduced the affordable auto, he also introduced the production line, a new technology that divided manufacturing into simple, repetitive operations. At first, people worked the assembly line, for almost everyone had the capability to do simple, low-tech repetitive operations, and the good salaries and benefits that Ford paid served to increase the market. So its affect was not noticed.

But in the late 1930's, with the advent of primitive robotics that could do some of the low-tech operations, the effects began to be noticeable. And, as robotics improved, fewer and fewer workers were needed to produce an automobile, or any other production line product. In candy factories, for example, once thousands of workers produced a hundred thousand candy bars a day, but today less than a hundred workers produce a half million a day.

But the decline was still slow for the control systems of the early robotics were clumsy and this limited the tasks robots could do. But, in the middle of the last century, digital computers burst on to the scene to change the pace. Computers did trigger a lot of new high-tech jobs, but they also made possible ever more clever robots capable in some cases of totally replacing humans.

Then in the 1960's, computerized robots began to really swallow even high-tech jobs by the millions. By 1980 they had replaced so many humans in the workplace, shrinking the market for products to such an extent, that business began to feel the effect. And, as sales fell, business began to lay off more and more workers; and unemployment became a serious and ever growing problem, creating a steady stream of economic recessions.

As the economy has ebbed since the 80's, governments have cut business taxes to help businesses survive, and borrowed more and more large amounts of money to increase domestic and defense spending to create jobs lost to robots. But, to control their rising national debt, governments had to also impose severe austerity programs. These eliminated government jobs and reduced educational and other social service budgets, and reduced market demand.

But then the advent of a worldwide banking "bubble" that allowed people to purchase with borrowed money beyond their means made it appear for the rest of the 20th century that the monetary system was still viable, when, in fact, it was being systematically undermined by the growing development of ever more efficient robots creating unemployment and shrinking the market.

Then, in 2008 when the banking "bubble" burst, we discovered, without the banking "bubble," there isn't sufficient market demand in a normal market to keep everyone working. It's true there may still be a few more bubbles in the future to keep things moving, but the truth is the monetary system is in an accelerating downslide with no permanent relief in sight.

According to Bureau of Labor Statistics data, one out of three manufacturing job, about six million factory jobs, have been lost since the end of the Great Depression. About as many people work in manufacturing jobs today as did at the end of the Depression, at a time when the American population was half of what it is now. With all those jobs gone, the market has shrunk easily by a third of what it was fifty years ago.

Look at the facts. The world market has shrunk to the point that the GDP of major industrial nations like Japan, England, and the United States is stagnating. This forces their governments to cut taxes even further, and to borrow more huge sums to stay afloat. And, to reduce the growth of debt, they institute even more severe austerity programs that create more unemployment that further shrinks the market.

There are still job openings, but they are high tech-jobs beyond the education or the mental capability of a large segment of society. And, with the austerity programs cutting educational budgets, people that could be educated to take the jobs can't afford the expense. So, many of the unemployed have taken part-time work at low wages to survive, which doesn't help the market much, and many even in the middle class expect to be permanently exiled from the economy.

And, since it is the history of technology to advance exponentially, low-tech jobs will disappear exponentially in all sectors of the economy – including mining, construction, retail sales, banking, the armed services, police, and fire fighting – all of which have traditionally been heavy employers of low-tech workers.

For example, the Wall Street Journal announced just today that the world's largest bookseller is installing robots to fill orders in its warehouse. In the past the firm hired thousands of workers to cruise through football-field warehouses to pick items from the shelves. Now the new robots do the work including locating the items, the packaging, and printing the receipts.

As MIT economists Brynjolfsson and McAfee noted in their e-book, *The Race Against the Machine,* examples of human beings being exiled are growing at an ever alarming speed and threatening almost every possible job. Even the factories that build the robots in Japan use robots that work night and day in the dark building other robots. I'm sure robots will always need people to tend them, but it seems it won't be in many areas.

As a result of this invasion there is now an estimated 20% to 30% unemployment among Hispanics and Blacks in the United States; and, in some places, 48% of young people between the ages of 18 and 28 are without jobs. Today 30% of the population receives food stamps, 50% of people live in multi-generational homes, college graduates, staggering under enormous student loans, are moving in with parents on graduation, and an estimated 30% of unrelated adults are doubling up. And experts see no relief in sight.

To add to the problem, shrinking markets have caused business to increase the pressure upon Congress to reduce the power of unions to reduce salaries and eliminate pension plans – all of which lowers the amount of money workers have to spend to buy the products produced by business – thereby shrinking the market even further, prompting more layoffs. Meanwhile the schoolmen are very quiet, for they don't know what's going on.

To really get a picture of how much the monetary system has declined, we need to compare attitudes of people and the schoolmen in the 1960's with their attitude today. In the 60's everyone was looking forward to ever growing prosperity and an increase in the middle classes. Europeans were developing a new generous social system. Today we despair for our children's future, and we can all see the growth of national debt and sovereign bankruptcy haunting more societies than we'd like to think.

This change is to a large extent the result of the steady advance of robotics, and we can't stop the advance because the monetary system is a profit-driven system, and, since fewer human employees means an increase in the profit for the owners of business, the monetary system will pressure business to steadily increase robotics. The monetary system is pushing its own decline.

And, worse, the advance of any technology is not linear, but exponential, and we are only somewhere at the beginning of the exponential curve, and just now entering the twilight of the monetary system. With this advance in robotic technology, if we continue to use the monetary system, all we can expect is ever increasing national debt and unemployment until the monetary system becomes so untenable that either we'll have a social revolution or the monetary system itself will collapse.

But there's no reason for despair, for we'll discover in this book that, contrary to what the schoolmen would have us believe, the ancient monetary system isn't the only system or the best system society can use to govern its economy. We'll discover science is responsible for the decline of the monetary system, and, if we create a new econoscience now while we're still muddling in the old system, the new science will quickly discover a viable and interesting alternative.

In the following pages, guided by the scientific method introduced in Francis Bacon's *Novum Organum* – the seminal work that guided

John Locke to develop modern political science and to discover political democracy – we'll follow the path blazed by Locke and together discover the new economic system that, if we choose to develop it, could create the dawn of a new era of both political and economic democracy where everyone enjoys a new level of prosperity created by man and machine working together.

Francis Bacon

*"I supply the mind with such rules and guidance that it may in every case apply itself aptly to the nature of things."*

# II
# How to Discover a
# New Economic System

**B**acon opens the *Novum Organum* with the important observation that, despite what we may like to believe, man doesn't invent things or behaviors. He merely manipulates things and behaviors that already exist in nature in a crude form to make them more suitable for our purposes.

*"Man, being the servant and interpreter of nature, can do and understand so much and so much only as he has observed in fact or in*

*thought of the course of nature; beyond this he neither knows anything nor can do anything. . . Towards the effecting of works, all that man can do is to put together or put asunder natural bodies. The rest is done by nature working within."*

Bacon then goes on to observe that, if we want to discover an alternative system of behavior that will advance human progress, we should begin by searching human behavior, past and present, for some *natural* behavior that fits the new goal, especially one that society rejected long ago as so clumsy and difficult as to be *impossible* to use in a sophisticated society.

*"As originally discovered they are commonly rude, clumsy, and shapeless, afterwards (with the help of man) they can acquire new powers and more commodious arrangements and constructions, but men sooner leave the study and pursuit of them, and turn to something else than arrive at the ultimate perfection of which they are capable. . . For the mind longs to spring up to positions of higher generality, that it may find rest there; and so after a little while wearies of experiment."*

Then, Bacon recommends that, when we find such a *natural* behavior, we must force ourselves to ignore the old decision, and all the logic schoolmen have used since to justify it. Then, with a clear mind, we must go back and reconsider whether the difficulties of the *natural* behavior could be overcome with modern technology, so the system could be used in a sophisticated society.

*"No one has yet been found so firm of mind and purpose as to resolutely compel himself to sweep away all theories and common notions, and to apply the understanding, thus made fair and even, to a fresh examination of the facts. Thus it happens that human knowledge, as we have it, is a mere medley and ill-digested mass, made up of much credulity and much accident, and also of the childish notions which we at first imbibed."*

**JOHN LOCKE,** the 17th century English philosopher, recognizing that English society was not advancing under the political oligarchy that ruled England and Europe by the Grace of God, followed Bacon's advice. He examined history for a *naturally* occurring secular political behavior that had been rejected long ago by society as so clumsy and difficult to organize that it was assumed *impossible* to be used in a sophisticated society.

He selected the political commonwealth or republican system that had *naturally* developed in ancient Greece and Rome; and that those societies had rejected as too clumsy and difficult to organize to use in its expanding political empire. They chose, instead, an oligarchy headed by an emperor supposedly anointed by the "divine hand" of a god, because it was easier to organize than the complex commonwealth and made the leaders more rich and powerful.

In his *Second Treatise on Government* Locke swept aside the rejection of the republican system, and the logic schoolmen like Filmer had written justifying the rejection, and concluded that, with modern 17th century technology, it would be quite possible to use a republican political system in the sophisticated and growing English Empire. Of course, he had to flee England to save his neck.

English schoolmen, accustomed to thousands of years of oligarchy, considered Locke's conclusion that common peasants could self-govern politics in a sophisticated expanding empire as *impossible*, and rejected his work as the product of an unripened mind. So Locke's theory of organizing a nation as a republic languished in England as theoretical nonsense for a century.

*"By far the greatest obstacle to the progress of science and the undertaking of new tasks and provinces therein is found in this – that men despair and think things impossible . . . that when they reach a certain point and condition they can advance no further and, if therefore anyone believes or promises more, they think this comes of an ungoverned and unripened mind."*

But a few decades later, English colonists in America, separated from the English oligarchy by a vast ocean, and well aware of Locke's theory, found it quite *natural* to organize themselves into 13 political commonwealths. By the 1770's these colonies had *experimentally* created sophisticated and interrelated politically self governing systems and called a Continental Congress to exchange ideas.

Then, in 1776, when the English oligarchy attempted to tax the colonies without providing them representation in Parliament, the 13 colonies joined together and declared their political independence. To the English oligarchy's surprise, the 13 commonwealths were well enough organized to field a ragtag army under George Washington, and chase the English and their sophisticated army out of the colonies.

The colonies then formed The United States, and the founders, men like Adams, Franklin, Jefferson, and Madison, but not Hamilton, students of Locke's political science, converted his theory and even his words into the Constitution and Bill of Rights. Jefferson wrote in his later years that he considered "Bacon, Locke and Newton were three of the most important men who ever lived."

The new political commonwealth or republic then put Locke's theory to the test, and, despite the fact that Hamilton, the first Secretary of the Treasury, managed to organize the nation's economy as an economic oligarchy, the experiment proved it was quite possible to use a political commonwealth in a sophisticated and expanding nation. It was so successful, in fact, that most European nations eventually adopted a political commonwealth or democracy.

And the very fact that the first political commonwealth or democracy that used Locke's discovery, with Bacon's guidance, is now the oldest, most continuous and most successful political government in history, is a credit to Bacon, and verifies his view that systems founded on *natural* behaviors tend to grow and prosper, but systems based upon unnatural behaviors tend to stagnate and languish.

*"Signs also are to be drawn from the increase and progress of systems and sciences. For what is founded on nature grows and increases; while what is founded on opinion varies but increases not."*

John Locke
Discoverer of How to Create
Political and Economic Democracy

# III
# Discovering a New Economic System

Following in Locke's footsteps, we'll now search man's behavior for a *naturally* occurring system of economic production and trade that doesn't use money, and that has been rejected by society as so clumsy and difficult to organize as to be *impossible* to use in a sophisticated society, and we will stick to facts and reject the opinions of schoolmen.

We can start with the historic fact pointed out by Locke that there were many very sophisticated societies with an economy producing and trading before money was invented. For example, biblical Mesopotamia had a sophisticated and extensive empire before money was invented, and the ancient Egyptians produced the pyramids and operated their extensive empires before money was invented. In fact, historians tell us there were lots of sophisticated empires in the old world before the monetary system was developed about 700BC.

And, for a more recent and historically confirmed example, the highly sophisticated Aztec, Mayan and Inca empires were built without the use of money, and the Spanish conquistadors reported their cities were in many ways as sophisticated and prosperous as cities in Europe. And it's important to note, as soon as the conquistadors introduced the monetary system, the Indians lost access to their resources and sunk into abject poverty.

And, we must also note the important fact that all of these societies that prospered before the invention of money; did so with very primitive communication, accounting, and organizational technology. They didn't even enjoy the use of a practical written language. We can only imagine what they might have accomplished with modern electronic communication, accounting, and organizational technology.

Locke, in his *Second Treatise, Chapter V, Of Property,* gives us an exhaustive description of how the moneyless economies worked. He notes that, before societies invented money, people had free access to the earth's resources, and made private property out of those resources with their labor. And, in the absence of money, people were not inclined to create more private property than they could use before it spoiled. As for trading goods and services, he found people used simple barter.

But, Locke notes, the appearance of the monetary system granting permanent unlimited power to the holder totally corrupted the system, for people then began to accumulate more than they needed, and the economic injustice we find today began. Locke dwells exhaustively on the subject, but I'll quote a few paragraphs to provide an idea of the theme of his findings.

*"And thus it is very easy to conceive how labor could at first begin a title of property in the common things of nature, and how the spending it upon our uses bounded it. So that there could then be no reason of quarrelling about title, or any doubt about the largeness of possession it gave.*

*"Right and convenience went together, for as a man had a right to all he could employ his labor upon, so he had no temptation to labor for more than he could make use of . . . it was useless, as well as dishonest to carve for himself too much, or take more than he needed.*

*"Thus in the beginning no such thing as money was anywhere known. Find out something that has the use and value of money amongst his neighbors, you shall see the same man will begin presently to enlarge his possessions."*

In making this observation Locke swept aside the opinions of schoolmen who lauded money as the "grease" of the economy. Locke found that the invention of money didn't help the flow of the economy – it corrupted the democratic economy intended by nature. Bacon, if faced with these facts, would say if man wants a system that will grow and improve, he needs to go back and scientifically develop the natural organization of the economy as it existed *before* the invention of money.

Bacon would point out that the monetary system is not a *natural* system. It does not occur in nature. No animal uses it except man, for it is wholly a product of man's imagination. He'd note that the opinion that money has any value is not a fact, it is merely an *opinion* of mankind that is not reflected anywhere in nature. So, Bacon would tell us, if man continues to use the monetary system, it will not bode well for mankind, because systems based on opinion may vary but they do not grow or improve. Only natural systems grow and improve.

*"Nature to be commanded must be obeyed . . . Toward the effecting of works, all that man can do is put together or put asunder natural bodies. The rest is done by nature working within."*

*"For what is founded on nature grows and increases, while what is founded on opinion varies but increases not. . . The arts founded on nature and the light of experience . . . at first rude, then convenient, afterwards adorned, are at all times advancing."*

So, returning to Locke, we find he not only discovered an alternative to political oligarchy, he also discovered an alternative to economic oligarchy. But he obviously decided that 17th century Englishmen were only sufficiently educated, and the technology of political communication and organization were only well enough advanced, that England could develop and use the republican system of self-government to replace its political oligarchy. So in his *Second Treatise* he completely described how to do so. The rest of course is political history.

However, Locke must have believed that in the 17th century the level of education of the people and economic communication and organizational technology were not well enough advanced to be able to create an economic democracy to replace economic oligarchy. So, like a good scientist, Locke merely reported his findings that the invention of the monetary system had corrupted the *natural* economic behavior of man without further comment, and left the creation of economic democracy to the future.

Today, however, we'll discover that the level of education and the technology to develop the natural economic system that existed before the invention of money does exist. Locke found that before the invention of money there were only *three* things necessary to operate a sophisticated economy – *labor, organization,* and *resources* – and we'll find that modern society has all three ingredients highly developed and readily available to develop the natural economic system that existed before the adoption of money.

In the following chapters we'll address each one of the three ingredients separately, and end with a good idea of what it will take to create an economic democracy with readily available education and organizational technology to replace the monetary system, and put an end to the inefficiency, instability and injustice we have in the monetary system. We'll discover that we have already at hand all we need to create a new era of economic and political democracy.

*"Noble inventions may be lying at our very feet, and yet mankind may step over without seeing them . . . Such is the infelicity and unhappy disposition of the human mind in this course of invention, that first it will not believe that any such thing can be found out; and when it is found out, cannot understand how the world should have missed it so long."*

*"And this very thing may be justly taken as an argument of hope; namely there is a great mass of inventions still remaining which . . . through the transferring, comparing, and applying of those inventions already known, by the help of science, new inventions may be deduced and brought to light."*

# IV
# Self-Governing Labor

*"It is not moneys that are the sinews of fortune; it is the sinew and steel of men's minds, wits, courage, audacity, resolution, temper, industry and the like."*

Schoolmen will argue that, even if we could get access to resources and have the necessary organization technology, we could never expect ordinary people to self-govern a sophisticated modern economy. They insist that society needs the money barons and the profit motive to guide and drive people in a sophisticated economy. The great fault of scholasticism is it has no faith in humanity.

*"The philosophy now in vogue embraces and cherishes certain tenets, the purpose of which is to persuade men that nothing difficult, nothing by which nature may be commanded and subdued, can be expected from human labor . . . Which things if they be noted accurately tend wholly to the unfair circumspection of human power, and a*

*deliberate and factitious despair; which not only disturbs the auguries of hope, but also cuts the sinews and spur of industry, and throws away the chances of experience itself, and all for the sake of having their art thought perfect, and for the miserable vain glory of making it believed that whatever has not yet been discovered and comprehended can never be discovered or comprehended hereafter."*

But, again, if we compel ourselves to put these scholastic notions aside and look at the facts, we will discover the money barons and the profit motive have nothing to do with production and distribution. Most money barons haven't the foggiest notion what goes on in the production and distribution of goods and services. They are only interested in the manipulation of money. Production of real wealth is merely a secondary consideration done only if it will make money.

The production and distribution of goods and services are left to people motivated by pride of workmanship, pleasure of working with others on productive projects, and people capable of self-governing their economic behavior. The people are not directed by money barons or driven by the profit motive – not just a few here and there – but literally the millions of people working every day in the economy.

We must note that in all vital areas of our economy where we want to avoid the corruption that comes with using money, we forbid the use of money during working hours, and rely upon well developed organization and people motivated by a sense of duty, pride of workmanship, and the pleasure of working with others as a team. In fact we can even say that the internal operation of all private business and government functions without money barons or the profit motive during the production and distribution of the real wealth of goods and services.

And our far flung armed forces function in a hundred and fifty nations without needing a monetary system. They all function on the sense of duty of the soldiers and sailor, and good military organization. Anyone demanding money to do something would wind up in jail or court-martialed and dishonorably discharged.

Take the specific example of the crew of a large aircraft carrier, nothing less than a huge self-contained modern city with hospitals, workshops, housing, food services, and many other working interactions. The crew functions often for long voyages on a sense of duty, pride of working together, and a well-developed military organization.

And, for an example of more extensive people working without a monetary system, we can point to the operation of World War II, where millions of men and women slogged across Europe and Asia, constantly risking their lives. The soldiers, sailors, and marines storming the beaches on D-Day didn't work for financial gain. They did it out of a sense of duty, pride of workmanship, and good military organization. So the facts reveal that people do produce without using or being driven by money.

So when the schoolmen talk about the need for money barons and the profit motive, they are not referring to production and distribution for the money barons have no interest in such things. They are referring to the operation of the monetary system that, of course, needs money barons and the profit motive, because that is what it is all about. It's not about production of goods and services.

But, if we brush aside the opinions of the schoolmen, and examine the facts, we find that we have available the first ingredient that Locke tells us is needed to operate a moneyless economy. We have all the highly educated self- governing and self-motivate *labor* we'll ever need on hand and readily available to create an economic democracy. In the next chapter we'll go back to the facts and we'll see that we also have available Locke's second ingredient – the ability to *organize* society for production and distribution in a sophisticated moneyless economic democracy.

# IV
## Organization Technology

Today, we easily have the organizational technology to mobilize labor for any purpose. We proved that in WWII. Starting from the economic doldrums of the Great Depression, when unemployment was nearly 25% and the production of goods and services at 50% of capacity, we suddenly organized an economy with full employment and production of goods and services unequaled in human history.

Let's sketch the organization that we developed in WWII when we passed in a matter of days from an economic depression where we didn't have any money to even pave our roads, to an economy that in a few months began to produce airplanes, guns, ships food, and housing in unbelievable quantities. There were huge convoys of ships leaving our harbors everyday loaded with goods, and everyone was working in factories that were producing 24/7.

We'll see in detail how we shifted from near financial bankruptcy in December 1941 to a wartime economy in 1942 – not because we found any money – but because we were threatened with extinction by Japan and Germany. I was there and I can testify it was a magical economic awakening. Like every other combatant in WWII, we simply ignored the lack of money.

And it was no flash in the pan for after the war my generation here and in Japan and Europe had leaders like Roosevelt, Truman, and Eisenhower who kept us ignoring the cries of despair and hand wringing of the schoolmen to produce an era of social prosperity unequaled in all of human history.

As for the schoolmen, they haven't the foggiest notion how the wartime and post war prosperity happened. And it is noteworthy that they don't bother studying it either to find out how it happened. They simply dismiss it as some kind of financial trick that never happened for nothing in their lexicon of monetary rules suggests it possible. And so, because we have no econoscience to study and document such experience, I'll have to sketch it from memory.

**I. Planning:** The first step in any war is to create a planning board made up of experts in all disciplines to scientifically organize society's resources and mobilize the manpower and know-how. This board of econoscientists would be made up of political scientists, business organizers, production engineers, lawyers, and every other discipline involved in the production and distribution of goods and services.

I can't stress too much the importance of this planning board and its subsidiaries, for it had the makings of an econoscience. If we had nurtured and allowed it to blossom, the world might be a different place today for they dealt with production, and ignored money for they had a deadly war to win. Unfortunately a generation later the schoolmen managed to take over and go back to spinning webs of empty logic, and allow all the experience of WWII to go to waste. What a pity.

*"The logic now in use serves rather to fix and give stability to the errors which have their foundation in commonly received notions than to help the search after truth. So it does more harm than good."*

**II. Organization:** The planners no doubt would form a new holding corporation, and give the corporation the power to *expropriate* essential

51

industrial corporations that already exist, and annex them as corporate subsidiaries. Each subsidiary would be run by a plant manager and his or her designers and production and distributions engineers and workers.

Each citizen of the society would receive one inalienable lifetime share in the holding corporation, making it effectively a corporate economic commonwealth. Each area of the society would elect a member of the Board of Directors of the holding corporation for a given term, and that body would elect the CEO.

The Board, made up of lawyers, production and distribution experts, and so forth, would create the operating rules and regulations of the commonwealth and enforce them, and the minutes of all meetings of the Board and all the rules and regulations would be posted daily on the internet.

The Board of Directors of the subsidiary corporations would be elected by the workers of the subsidiary, who would hold equal shares in both the subsidiary and the holding corporation. Also users of the materials produced, and the Board of the holding corporation would elect Directors of the subsidiary.

The subsidiary Board would appoint a CEO, and set wages based upon the value of the work involved according to a formula supplied by the holding corporation. Everyone involved in the organization would in some way be part of the production and distribution of goods and services needed by the economic commonwealth.

**II. Resources:** The citizen-owned holding corporation would also have the power to *expropriate* the essential resources required to produce the war materials needed. The holding corporation would allocate the resources to each subsidiary necessary for it to reach its quota of production. Thus, elected representatives of the citizens would effectively control society's resources.

This is an important point for this was wartime and, unlike in a peacetime monetary economy, society's government didn't need the permission of anyone to appropriate the necessary resources. And the government paid for the resources by simply printing money and paying for them with inflated money at a price set by the government. Society didn't allow the oligarchy to hold society ransom during the war and impede production as in peacetime.

As we shall see in detail in the next chapter, this ability of society to have unrestricted access to resources was the key to the enormous production during the WWII years. In peacetime individuals and society may have an idea and desire to produce something, but they didn't have the money to get the permission of the oligarchy to have access to the resources, and the goods never get produced. In short, the key to unlimited production is access to unlimited resources.

**IV. Conflict Resolution:** A Board of Appeals would be established with the duty of resolving all conflicts between corporations, between workers and corporations, between users and corporations, and any other dispute that arises in the commonwealth. The decisions of the Board would be reviewable by the civil courts of the political commonwealth.

**V. Economic Rights:** Every citizen would have an inalienable right to be employed at a fair wage by the commonwealth industries. Robots would perform as many jobs in production as desired to reduce the time citizens had to work, but without reducing worker's wages as their hours diminished. This would meet the goal of organizing an economic system to employ modern technology for the benefit of the people.

**VI. Medium of Exchange:** In order to produce and distribute goods and services in such an extended system would require a *medium of exchange*. But it is here that we'll make a great change, for the power granted by the new medium of exchange would be severely *limited* to prevent the injustice that Locke notes occurs with the use of the *unlimited* power of money. Here, too, we'll use electronic technology not available in WWII.

Workers would be paid with electronic *credits* on a sliding scale according to the value of their participation as now, and the credits would be used by the citizen to purchase goods and services from the system storehouses and service units. Or they could be used to purchase personal services from individuals, and those individuals could then use the credits at the storehouses and service units.

However, since the credits would bestow economic power upon the holder, the power of the credits would be *limited* as to term. They would expire at the end of each month, at which time able bodied citizens in the commonwealth would be required to go back to work to earn more credits for purchases during the new term. Children, students, the disabled and retirees would receive credits each term free.

John Locke would note that this limitation of power effectively restores the natural safeguard he noted occurred before the introduction of money. It effectively prevents people from taking more than they need, and the new organization of the economy provides assurance to people that they don't have to hoard, because they will always be able to earn next month's needs. I'll repeat Locke's observation.

*"Right and convenience went together, for as a man had a right to all he could employ his labor upon, so he had no temptation to labor for more than he could make use of . . . it was useless, as well as dishonest to carve for himself too much, or take more than he needed."*

Locke would also note the limitation will end the controversy that goes on in the monetary system as to whether a person is pulling his weight. With the limitation every able bodied person will be required to go to work each month to earn his keep. If he doesn't work he will starve. Let's repeat the observation of Locke.

*"And thus it is very easy to conceive how labor could at first begin a title of property in the common things of nature, and how the spending it upon our uses bounded it. So that there could then be no reason of quarrelling*

*about title, or any doubt about the largeness of possession it gave."*

And the credits would not be physical in form. They would be electronically deposited at a central bank organized by the commonwealth, and spent by the workers with a debit card. Thus, *transparency* so important to democracy is established, and society will always know how much credit is in the system, where it is, and how it is being used – important information that will serve to regulate production, set wages, and prevent economic crime such as the sale of drugs.

As for the "big brother" argument, we must hasten to note it is not government that would know a person's business. It will be society at large. Everyone will know what's going on and where the individual stands in the system. People may not like having everyone knowing their business, but the dissemination of information into society at large is the keystone of any democratic organization.

In the monetary system we do have to keep our finances a secret because there are people lurking everywhere ready to steal money or interfere with business. In the new system there won't be a need to steal, for one's needs are readily available by joining in the production of wealth, everyone's business would benefit the entire society, and the new medium of exchange, because of its term limit, can't be hoarded.

Thus there'd be no advantage to stealing, and, since everyone is sharing in the production of every business, it would be foolish to interfere in any business. So corruption and injustice would be limited by the simple act of *limiting the term* of the medium of exchange. This is the neat trick society has learned over the three hundred years of political democracy. Limit the term of any power issued by society, and corruption and injustice is automatically limited.

Francis Bacon would put it another way. He'd say it is by the simple act of restoring the organization of the economy to the way nature intended that we'd be correcting the corruption and injustice created by the introduction of the *unnatural* money system. By abiding by nature, he'd say, we'd be creating a system that can grow and improve with use. Let me repeat two of Bacon's succinct observations.

*"The subtlety of nature is greater many times over than the subtlety of our senses and understanding."*

*"For what is founded on nature grows and increases, while what is founded on opinion varies but increases not."*

As for the exchange of goods and services within the corporation, the medium of exchange could be credits or by requisition as is the case in industry, government and the military. As for the exchange of goods and services between the corporation and private enterprise, or with foreign enterprise, that would be handled strictly by highly organized barter, for the use of money would be illegal in and by the commonwealth.

As we can see this system would have all the positive effects of a monetary system, but, because it has a *limited* term, it would have none of the detrimental effects. It would be an effective medium of exchange, and an effective way to reward good behavior, but it would not provide the holder with the raw unlimited power of money. And, because, unlike the other organization technology copied from WWII or already in use, the system is new and untested, it needs to be experimentally developed and tested before adoption.

**VII. Accounting:** There would be a universal electronic point-of-sale accounting system. As soon as something is sold at the system market place or used in production, the manufacturing subsidiary would be notified to produce to replace the item. Thus, once an inventory is set up by the elected Directors as determined by supply and demand, the inventory would automatically and accurately be maintained.

**VIII. Application:** The commonwealth system would only apply to the production, distribution and service operation of the essential industries. Once workers get credits, they could do what they wish with them. They could use them to purchase goods and services at the company storehouse, sell them for money or gold, or they could even use them to gamble at casinos.

Why would the new organization only apply to the production side of the economy and not the entire economy? The answer is that society should insure that everyone has an inalienable right to participate and to share in the production of society's economy, but it would be an infringement of privacy to control what a person does with his share honestly gained by his or her labor. (However it might be a good idea to eliminate cash, and use only debit card transactions that could be monitored to reduce corruption and crime.)

And the commonwealth organization would not necessarily include the entire economy. For example, society could create a commonwealth system for the unemployed so they could earn their keep with their labor. This would take the load off the monetary system, and help it function more efficiently, and even help to prolong its usefulness.

In short, we'd end with a hybrid system. The commonwealth would produce essential goods and services, and the monetary system could produce non-essentials, and continue to be used on the entire consumer side of the economy. Such a hybrid system would probably be necessary because some people are not going to willingly dispense with money even if they have to trade with gold or beads.

**IX. Trade:** The commonwealth would trade with the private sector and other societies only by barter, even if the outsiders remain on the monetary system. There would be a constitutional separation of the monetary system and the commonwealth, for, as Locke noted, the introduction of money in any way is an invitation to corruption of the natural justice of a commonwealth.

**X. Operation:** Once set up, computers would determine the production and salary schedules, and the number and type of workers necessary. Ultimately, robots would do most of the work, and people would only be required to labor the amount of time necessary for them to earn the credits to supply their needs.

*"Meantime, let no man be alarmed at the multitude of particulars, but let this rather encourage him to hope . . . for this road has an issue in the open ground and not far off. The other has no issue at all, but endless entanglement."*

**As we can see** from my thumbnail sketch, the physical organization of a commonwealth would be simple. It would be designed to *limit* economic power, with the term of the elected Board of Directors limited, and the term of the medium of exchange limited. And, since we already have hundreds of years of experience in a political commonwealth, and know the importance of limiting power, there is nothing new required in that aspect.

And there's nothing new about the physical organization of a commonwealth. It's merely a reorganization of well-developed already existing corporate structure with the corporate stock owned equally by the people, and the corporation operated for the people, with the goal of using modern science to benefit the life, liberty and the pursuit of happiness of the people.

And we know from experience in WWII that, if we don't worry about money, and put the available self-motivated labor and the modern technology of production organization to work, society has the capacity to bury the world in goods and services. In twenty years with our supply of self-governing labor and organizational technology, the world could easily produce enough goods and services to win a War on Poverty.

But the problem is we still lack the third ingredient for production and distribution — society still lacks free access to *resources.* Society's resources are by agreement the private property of the money barons, and they hold society ransom. Thus society's access to self governing labor and organizational technology are useless without access to resources. And herein lays the problem that has to be resolved before society can put its labor and organization to work to create a moneyless economic democracy.

# V
## Free Access to Resources:
## The Problem to Be Resolved

All forms of commonwealth or democratic organization require access to resources, and long ago in its childhood, society gave up its right of access to its political and economic resources, and allowed individuals to legitimately claim them as private property. Political and money barons took control of the resources and began to demand ransom from society.

Two hundred and fifty years ago, schoolmen told society that the only way to get access to resources is to get the oligarchy – the political and economic barons – to approve of the project. They had no idea that society has any right to access to the world's resources. As far as they were concerned the ownership of the resources by the land and economic barons was carved in stone and unchangeable.

But in 1776 the American people, after much thought, decided to stand up for their rights, revoked the agreement regarding political resources, and took control of their political assets to form a political commonwealth or democracy. Today political scientists have replaced the schoolmen, and they assure the world that a society has an inalienable right to access to political resources and will help any society to take charge and run those resources.

But American society did not stand up for its rights concerning economic resources, and allowed them to remain private property. So, in 1776, America merely replaced *land* barons with *money* barons, and tyranny shifted from politics to economics. Today schoolmen assure us the money barons have a right carved in stone to own society's economic resources and there's nothing legally we can do about it and society agrees.

*"But by far the greatest obstacle to the progress of science and to the undertaking of new tasks and new provinces therein, is found in this – that men despair and think things impossible."*

The decision to revoke the old agreement of access to its political resources in 1776 was a traumatic move for society, for The English Lords and King who owned the different American colonies were deprived of their property without just compensation. The same thing happened when the various colonies in Asia, Africa and the Middle East declared their independence, and the foreign owners were deprived of their property without compensation.

But, in order to create an economic commonwealth or democracy, society will have to get free access to its economic resources and means of production. If society decides to create only a limited economic democracy to provide jobs only for the unemployed, society could do as it did in WWII and print money and pay the owners in inflated dollars. That would work on a small scale.

However, if society decides to go whole hog and convert the entire production side of the economy to an economic democracy, it will need to revoke the long standing agreement regarding economic resources, and take control of them without compensating the owners as they did their political resources in 1776. Classically societies are slow to take such steps. Jefferson mentions the situation.

*"Prudence, indeed, will dictate that Governments long established should not be changed for light and transient causes; and accordingly all experience hath shewn, that mankind are more disposed to suffer, while evils are sufferable, than to right themselves*

*by abolishing the forms to which they are accustomed. But when a long train of abuses and usurpations, pursuing invariably the same Object evinces a design to reduce them under absolute Despotism, it is their right, it is their duty, to throw off such Government, and to provide new Guards for their future security."*

Unfortunately, we don't have much time to make such a monumental decision. Every year robots are pushing the monetary system closer to the brink. If we don't make the choice soon, growing unemployment and austerity programs will push the unemployed to possibly cataclysmic violence. We must change our economic government from the oligarchic monetary system to a new system of economic democracy before economic Armageddon.

**OF COURSE, OUR SCHOOLMEN** will say Russian society expropriated its economic resources and means of production in 1917 without compensating the owners, as have other societies, and the Russian Revolution and that of the other societies ended in tyrannical chaos. They tout this failure as proof that a commonwealth is *impossible;* solemnly implying that society must always suffer the inefficiency, instability and tyranny of oligarchy as "the best of all possible worlds."

Schoolmen simply don't believe man is capable of, or that he has any right to economic self government. Even those who tout economic revolution will insist a society turn over control of the resources to a central committee to act as oligarchs. None talk about replacing the monetary system and its *unlimited* power with an economic commonwealth where economic power is *limited*. They can't imagine a society without some form of oligarchy.

*"The philosophy now in vogue embraces and cherishes certain tenets, the purpose of which is to persuade men that nothing difficult, nothing by which nature may be commanded and subdued, can be expected from art or human labor . . . and all for the sake of having their art thought perfect, and for the miserable vain glory of making it believed that whatever has not yet been discovered and comprehended can never be discovered or comprehended hereafter."*

But, if we sweep aside the opinions of the schoolmen, and examine the facts, we'll see the Russian Revolution failed because it wasn't done scientifically. The Russian people had no plan, no prior experience in economic or political self-government, and, most important, they didn't abolish the monetary system when they expropriated their resources. They simply turned the resources over to the control of a central committee that used the resources to grow rich and more tyrannical than the private owners.

The American political revolution, on the other hand, succeeded where many other political revolutions had failed, because the revolution was done quite scientifically. The people had a half-century of experience in political self-government directed by Locke's detailed plan, and, when they took legitimate control of their political resources, they organized a political commonwealth to limit the power of its politicians to abuse the resources. Otherwise they'd have ended with another king and barons and the same tyranny.

So, in order to create an economic commonwealth, it is vitally necessary to do it scientifically. Society would need a definite plan of organization, a well-tested moneyless medium of exchange, at least some guidance of what to expect in economic self-government, and, most important, it needs to organize an economic democracy to limit the power of its economic leaders. Otherwise, leaders of society's economy would use the resources to grow rich and tyrannical as did the central committee in Russia.

In the old days, Bacon would have urged someone with the prestige of a John Locke to use the scientific method to investigate economic behavior, publish the findings, and then step aside to await informed leaders of society to use the information to start the ball rolling. That's how the American political revolution happened, but it took a full half-century of experimental preparation to get the job done.

Today that approach won't work. We're living in an advanced Age of Science, and the science of robotics is rapidly pushing the monetary system into obsolescence. Society doesn't have a half century to spare. The monetary system has already entered its twilight. We need to immediately create an econoscience to scientifically prepare for the transformation of our economy from a monetary oligarchy to a moneyless economic democracy while we're still able to muddle peacefully along in the old system.

Bacon and Locke, however, would warn any advocates of establishing an econoscience that there is a troublesome adversary awaiting anyone who speaks out against the monetary system. This adversary will resist even the organization of an econoscience, much less an investigation to develop an alternative for the monetary system. In the next chapter we'll reveal the troublesome adversary, and in the final chapter learn how Bacon and Locke would advise econoscientists to overcome the adversary.

Adam Smith
Chief apologist for Mammon

# VI
# The Troublesome Adversary

*"Neither is it to be forgotten that in every age science has had a troublesome adversary and hard to deal with; namely superstition and the blind and immoderate zeal of religion."*
*Francis Bacon*

B acon and Locke would tell us that economically society is still stuck in the medieval *Age of Faith.* They'd note the monetary system is not a secular human behavioral system. It is a well-organized and zealous idolatry centered upon the worship of money, or, as it is often referred to by other religions, the god Mammon. The world hasn't yet by any means moved into the Age of Science in economic behavior.

And it is a powerful idolatry, for Mammon is not an invisible spirit residing in some remote universe. Mammon is a physical idol we can hold in our hand, put in a safe, and we can constantly see it demonstrate its awesome power over people. And we are so deeply addicted to using its raw unlimited power, that, like all addicts, we are blind to the damage our use of the monetary system is doing to our civilization, and we can't imagine life deprived of the thrill of using it.

In the past, religious apologists warned us that Mammon was an evil agent of the Devil, with Timothy going so far as to write: "The love of money is the root of all evil." But, as Luther noted in his 95 Theses, even the Pope and the Church fathers fell under the influence of Mammon. Society eventually struck an uneasy bargain. If society worships God in Heaven on Sunday, it can worship Mammon the rest of the week without condemnation.

But in 1776, the very year political science was to begin its first formal experiment in political democracy, the English schoolman, Adam Smith, completely reversed the field. His *Wealth of Nations* declared that money isn't evil, but is the wonderful cause of all of man's prosperity. And, because it was written in the Age of Science, many hail the book as a product of the scientific enlightenment.

However, had Bacon been alive at the time, he'd have recognized Adam Smith as just another medieval schoolman writing an apology for money in the style and tradition of Aristotle. He would have warned us to beware of this kind of empty logic, for, not only is it useless, it clogs up the mind with circular arguments that end where they begin.

*"The logic now in use serves rather to fix and give stability to the errors which have their foundation in commonly received notion than to help the search after truth. So it does more harm than good."*

Bacon would have noted that Smith begins the *Wealth of Nations* by dividing the economy into qualitative categories of *land, labor, and capital,* just as Aristotle divided the physical universe into qualitative categories of *earth, air, fire and water.* He didn't divide it into its physical parts like a science.

*"The human understanding is of its own nature prone to abstractions and gives a substance and reality to things which are fleeting. But to resolve nature into abstractions is less to our purpose than to dissect her into parts, as did the school of Democritus which went further into nature*

*than the rest. Matter rather than forms should be the object of our attention, its configurations and changes of configuration, and simple action and law of action or motion, for forms are mere figments of the human mind.*

Then, like Aristotle, Bacon would note that Smith spins webs of logic around the categories, treating them as if they were the physical *base elements* of the economy, when they are nothing but empty qualitative categories created by the human mind.

*"The most conspicuous example of the first class was Aristotle, who corrupted philosophy by his logic; fashioning the world out of categories; assigning to the human soul the noblest of substances, a genus from words of the second intention."*

Then Bacon would note that Smith copies the panegyric schoolmen used to laud the faith-based political oligarchy. Their argument was that political prosperity is created by God whose "divine hand" anoints the king and lords to control the nation's politics, and, if the people have faith in God and do as they are told by the king and lords, the anointed will create the best of all possible political worlds.

In *The Wealth of Nations* Smith simply repeats the panegyric. He argues that economic prosperity is created by money, whose "invisible hand" anoints economic lords to control the nation's economy, and, if the people have faith in money, and do as they are told by the lords, the anointed will create the best of all possible economic worlds.

And Bacon would note that Smith, like all schoolmen, had little respect for humanity. Smith implies the sinew of prosperity is the "invisible hand" of money, and that mankind is merely a mindless laborer driven by greed. There are even passages in the *Novum Organum* that indicate that Bacon may have anticipated the appearance of an Adam Smith.

*"In their idle and most slothful conjectures, schoolmen ascribed to substances wonderful virtues and operations as to aim rather at admiration and novelty than at utility and fruit."*

*"It is not moneys that are the sinews of fortune; it is the sinew and steel of men's minds, wits, courage, audacity, resolution, temper, industry, and the like."*

*"The philosophies now in vogue embrace and cherish certain tenets, the purpose of which (if it be diligently examined) is to persuade men that nothing difficult, nothing by which nature may be commanded and subdued, can be expected from human labor . . . which tends wholly to the unfair circumscription of*

*human power, and to a deliberate and factitious despair; which not only disturbs the auguries of hope, but also cuts the sinews and spur of industry . . . and all for the sake of having their art thought perfect, and for the miserable vain glory of making it believed that whatever has not yet been discovered and comprehended can never be discovered or comprehended."*

*"Nor is it only of the systems now in vogue, or only of the ancient sects and philosophies that I speak; for many more plays of the same kind may yet be composed and in like artificial manner set forth; seeing that errors the most widely different have nevertheless causes for the most part alike."*

The point Bacon is making is that things like money or the other things Smith includes in his qualitative category of "capital" in reality have no magical powers. For Smith to tell us that "capital" has an "invisible hand" that anoints leaders, and causes them to lead society to prosperity is the useless nonsense typically produced by his scholastic method of thinking.

If man reacts to money or "capital," it comes from as an addictive aberration of man's mind, not a magical power of gold, silver, dollars, for these objects have no more power than a golden idol of Zeus or Athena. There is no such thing as an "invisible hand." That Smith in the Age of Science would write such medieval nonsense, or that modern schoolman would repeat it, merely illustrates how deeply we are stuck in the *Age of Faith* in economic thinking.

And, Bacon would note, as with all works of the scholastic schoolmen, Smith's *Wealth of Nations* is not about *how* *to* organize production, distribution, and services to create prosperity. It is a logical treatise about *where* prosperity comes from. Smith argues prosperity comes from – the "invisible hand" of money, and man only has to have faith and do as he is told. This information is of no benefit to creating prosperity. It is sterile of value.

*"By far the greater evil is that they make the quiescent principles wherefrom, and not the moving principles whereby things are produced, the object of their contemplation and inquiry. For the former tend to discourse, the latter to works."*

*"For they bring them into the view of the world so fashioned and masked, as if they were complete in all parts and finished . . . . It is nothing strange if men do not seek to advance things delivered to them as long since perfect and complete."*

And, Bacon would note, like all his fellow schoolmen, Smith wrote only about money's positives. He tells us at great lengths how the invisible hand of money has created all the prosperity in the nation. He didn't mention the system's woeful inefficiency, instability, and the corruption, crime and injustice that accompanies its use. According to Bacon he was following the scholastic method of ignoring negatives.

*"It is the peculiar and perpetual error of human logic to be more moved and excited by affirmatives than by negatives; whereas it ought properly to hold itself indifferently disposed towards both alike. Indeed in the establishment of any true axiom, the negative instance is the more forcible of the two."*

And, Bacon would note that, as with all religious *faith-based* systems, Smith's sect of "capitalism" was followed by Marx's sect of "socialism," agreeing with Smith that money was the cause of prosperity, but arguing that the other "means of production" included in the qualitative category of capital should be owned by the government, and the anointed better regulated.

And Lenin created the sect of "communism," agreeing with Smith that money is the cause of all prosperity, and the means of production should owned by the government, but arguing the anointed should be sent to Siberia, and their money taken over by a central committee as well. All of these "ism's or sects are the product of using the medieval method of thinking that dominates our economy.

*"For let a man look carefully into all that variety of which the arts abound, he will everywhere find endless repetitions of the same thing, varying in the method of treatment, but not new in substance , , , for it is fruitful of controversies but barren of works . . . and all the succession of schools is still a succession of masters and scholars, not of those who bring things to further perfection."*

And, Bacon would note, as with all such superstitious idolatry, the sects are constantly at odds, with conflicts often flaring into horrible and irrational wars. The conflict between capitalism and communism in the last century was like the Hundred Years War between Christian sects in Europe, often taking civilization to the brink of disaster.

And experience has taught us, ultimately, regardless of the sect that gains dominance, the economy always ends in the same oligarchy with a few of the anointed accumulating all the money power. No matter what sect controls the money in society,

society always ends with the same poverty and instability all accompanied by corruption and injustice.

**AND WE CAN SEE** for ourselves that our monetary system is faith-based for money only works if society has *faith* in the money god and its anointed; and falters whenever faith falters. The monetary system is all about having and keeping the faith. We appoint high priests as "keepers of the faith," who, in turn, employ an army of soothsayers to search the economy for, and to interpret, "signs" of faltering faith.

And we are constantly concerned about the level of faith, for we hate the "inflation" of money that comes from faltering faith. But the great mystery is the fact that "deflation" created by excessive faith is even worse. So our high priest must watch the signs and make sure faith is balanced somewhere between inflation and deflation.

And we know that, in order to maintain faith in money, the high priest must keep the amount of money in circulation in *short supply,* for our faith in money requires that it be kept rare like gold and silver. So, there's never enough money in circulation to allow everyone to prosper. Thus, to sustain faith in money, we condemn a third of our society, and most people in the third world, to struggle in poverty.

And the way we determine when to adjust the money supply is to watch the level of unemployment. If the number of people exiled from the economy exceeds 7% of the population, the High Priest orders more money issued. If it falls below 7%, they call for a reduction in the money supply. Thus, to maintain faith in money, we not only condemn millions to poverty, we exile millions from participating in their own economy.

So, as we can see, in the monetary system we don't have a goal of producing goods to end poverty. Our goal is to protect our faith in money. And, since money is kept in short supply to protect the faith, and production depends upon the money supply, production is also kept in short supply. As a result, while every advanced society has the capacity to produce enough goods to create full prosperity, all limit production to protect the faith in money.

As for the confusion we experience using the money system, it is created by our foolish notion that we can represent goods of *fleeting* value, with money of *fixed* value. In other words, we're foolishly attempting to represent apples with oranges, and as everyone knows this creates confusion. You can only accurately represent a thing of *fleeting* value with a thing of the same *fleeting* value.

**TODAY, OF COURSE,** even the schoolmen realize something is terribly wrong in the economy, but, notice, they *never, never blame the monetary system.* Instead, they blame the problems on the difficult nature of economics, the obscurity of economic problems, and, most important, the weakness of man's ability to understand economics. All end with the typical schoolman logical conclusion that it is *impossible* for man to create a stable economy providing prosperity for all, and that the economy will always cycle from boom to bust and back again.

*"For even they who lay down the law on all things so confidently, do still in their more sober moods fall to complaints of the subtlety of nature, the obscurity of things, and the weakness of the human mind . . . But not content to speak for themselves, whatever is beyond their own or their master's knowledge or reach, they set down as beyond the bounds of possibility."*

It is time, now that man has learned in politics that faith-based behavioral systems are always inefficient, unstable and accompanied by corruption and injustice; to realize the same holds true for economic behavioral systems. But we don't recognize the problem, because we don't want to recognize it. We're blindly entangled with the worship of money and so in love with using its raw and unlimited power that, like drug addicts, we can't imagine living without the thrill of using the object of our addiction.

And all of the webs of logic of Adam Smith, Karl Marx and Lenin, and our modern schoolmen, and the hundreds of newspaper and magazines dedicated to disputing logic about money and the 'isms, all serve to fix society in the Age of Faith and prevent us from developing an econoscience and moving economic behavior into the Age of Science.

*"As the sciences we now have do not help us in finding out new works, so neither does the logic which we now have help us in finding out new sciences. The logic now in use serves rather to fix and give stability to the errors which have their foundation in commonly received notions than to help the search after truth. So it does more harm than good."*

**BUT, IF WE CAN** overcome this blindness we'll recognize that the monetary system is a powerful primitive idolatry, and we can begin to understand why society adopted the monetary system long ago, and why we are so blind to the damage using a faith-based economic system is to society. And, too, we can see that advocates of a new econoscience can expect rejection that will come from the same troublesome class of adversaries that troubled advocates of every new science.

The *first* class is the vested interests, members of the anointed or central committee whose power over society rests on their position in the monetary system. This class can be physically dangerous, for it includes people who will stop at nothing to protect the monetary system to retain their source of power.

The *second* class is the devout worshippers of Mammon. These are people deeply addicted to the thrill and excitement of using the raw and unlimited power of money. Like all addicts, they devoutly believe life would be *impossible* without the addictive thrill of using the raw unlimited power of money, and are terrified by the thought of being deprived of the source of the thrill.

*"The idols and false notions which are now in possession of the human understanding, and have taken deep root therein, not only so beset men's mind that truth can hardly find entrance, but even after entrance is obtained, they will again at the very instauration of the sciences meet and trouble us, unless men forewarned of the danger fortify themselves as far as may be against their assaults."*

And the *third* class is the army of schoolmen who have spent their lives writing, teaching, and disputing the logic of the "isms" of monetary economics preaching that money has an "invisible hand" and especially those that preach that economic oligarchy creates "the best of all possible worlds." Some will welcome econoscience, but most will see it as a threat, and blindly try to block its acceptance at universities and seats of government. As Bacon always notes, it is this class that causes the most trouble.

*"Men become attached to certain particular sciences and speculations, either because they fancy themselves the author and inventors thereof, or because they have bestowed the greatest pains upon them and become most habituated to them. But men of this kind, if they betake themselves to philosophy and contemplations of a general character, distort and color them, in obedience to their former fancies."*

But, despite all the problems Mammon's worshipers might present, we have good reason for hope, because, fortunately, advocates of physics, medicine, and political science were faced with the same troublesome adversary, and they managed to survive and have their sciences flourish. In the next chapter we'll see how, guided by Bacon, they did so.

# VII
## Overcoming The
## Troublesome Adversary

*"Let there be two streams and two dispensations of knowledge and likewise two tribes or kindred of students in philosophy – tribes not alien to each other, but bound together by mutual service, in short – one method for the cultivation, and another for the invention of knowledge."*

Francis Bacon was not a scientist. He was a brilliant lawyer, the Chief Prosecutor of England, then Chief Judge, and a student of the Rules of Evidence used in the English Law Courts. In the *Novum Organum* he adapted those rules to the investigation of nature, and, of these, he considered the "hearsay" rule the most important and very foundation of the search for truth.

*"For I admit nothing but on the faith of eyes, or at least of careful and severe examination; so that nothing is exaggerated for wonder's sake, but what I state is sound and without mixtures of fables or vanity.*
*"Those who aspire not to guess and divine, but to discover and know, who propose not to devise mimic and create fabulous worlds of their own, but to examine and dissect the*

*nature of the very world itself; must go to the*
*facts themselves for everything. . .*
*"Lay it down once and for all as a fixed and*
*established maxim that the intellect is not*
*qualified to judge, except by means of*
*induction of fact, and induction in its*
*legitimate form."*

Bacon also recommended that all scientific investigation be conducted with the same decorum used in the English courtroom. And, while he insisted that all prior decisions made or reported by philosophers need to be checked and rechecked against experience or experiment, he urged scientists to treat the philosophers themselves with complete respect.

*"The honor of the ancient authors remains*
*untouched since the comparison I challenge is*
*not of wits or faculties, but of ways and*
*methods . . . to make a stand upon the ancient*
*way, and then look about us, and discover*
*what is the straight and the right way; and so*
*to walk in it."*

And, since the *Novum Organum* was published in 1620 while the world was still in the Age of Faith, and the physical world was seen from the religious viewpoint of view, and to publish any view that conflicted with religion was physically dangerous, Bacon advised advocates of science to present science as a "handmaiden" to religion, and to conduct all investigations quietly without comment.

*"But if the matter be truly considered, science is after the word of God the surest method against superstition, and the most approved nourishment for faith, and therefore is rightly given to religion as her most faithful handmaiden, for the one displays the will of God, and the other his power."*
*"It would be good that men in their innovations follow the example of time itself, which, indeed, innovates greatly, but quietly, and by degrees scarce to be perceived."*

The whole tenor of Bacon's *Novum Organum* is that science should investigate the behavior of the universe, select those behaviors it believes would be beneficial to mankind, work to improve them, publish its findings with a complete record of how they were made, and let society be the jury of how the findings are applied. He urged science to act only as a guide and never a judge.

*"A caution must be given the understanding against intemperance . . . This excess is of two kinds: the first being manifest in those who are ready in deciding, and render sciences dogmatic and magisterial; the other in those who deny that we can know anything, and so introduce a wandering kind of inquiry that leads to nothing . . .*

*"I have not sought, nor do I seek either to force or ensnare men's judgments, but I lead them to things themselves and the concordances of things, that they may see for themselves what they have, what they can dispute, what they can add and contribute to the common stock."*

Had Galileo read Bacon, he may not have gotten into his controversy fifteen years later with the Church, for the Church did not object to Galileo's finding about the heavens with his telescope. It only objected when he wrote a book ridiculing the biblical position concerning the solar system. Fortunately, the next scientific genius to come on the scene had read Bacon, carefully took his advice, and set the scene of a cordial relationship with religion.

**PHYSICS:** Isaac Newton, the virtual dictator of the London Society, the first organization dedicated to Bacon's memory, and the first dedicated to the advancement of science, was educated in a seminary. He always made it very clear that science was not in competition with religion, and tactfully deferred to religion when any conflict arose.

Of course this deferential attitude was safer two centuries ago, but it was also an honest attitude, for Newton found many aspects of the physical world far beyond physical science to explain. He felt, for science to assume it knows all would be as bad as religious writers assuming they know all.

And religion responded by supporting Newton's work. Universities in Europe, for the most part supported by religion, opened their doors to his findings even when they conflicted with the Bible. Ultimately, all European universities established departments of physics, and generally left physicists free to explore the behaviors of the physical world without interference. Of course, when religion objected, Newton always avoided argument.

*"The most beautiful system – the universe – could only proceed from the dominion of an intelligent and powerful being I call God . . . Tact is the art of making a point without making an enemy."*

**Astrophysics, unfortunately,** didn't enjoy the same relationship. Trouble began with the missteps of Galileo, but things were then patched up with religion by later astrophysicists. Einstein, for example, showed extreme tact and respect for the duality when he declared; "Science without religion is lame. Religion without science is blind."

And up until Einstein's death, religiously supported universities responded by accepting scientific theories of the universe even though they might disagree with scripture. But after the death of Einstein, the English astronomer Fred Hoyle became the spokesperson for astrophysics, and magisterially promoted his belief in a "steady state" universe that had no beginning or end.

This clearly conflicted with Genesis, but religion didn't really object until Hoyle publicly ridiculed Hubble's theory that the universe was created in a gigantic explosion, and is still expanding out into space, a theory that agrees with the story of Genesis. He laughingly referred to it as the "big bang."

The result was religion was furious, and religious leaders were able to get the scientific establishment to reject the "unified field theory" that had led astrophysicists to such enormous progress, and to adopt the "big bang" theory that agreed with Genesis. Today, most research money is spent to answer the question of *where* the universe came from, *where* it is going, and *how many* universes exist.

The result is that there hasn't been a new breakthrough in understanding of *what* the universe is made of, or *how* its behaviors are created since Einstein. Of course, there are still astrophysicists, but they are inhibited by their inability to correspond and discuss their ideas, for the establishment and the media are busy worrying about *where* the universe came from.

*"By far the greater evil is that they make the quiescent principles wherefrom and not the moving principles whereby things are produced the object of their inquiry."*

*"In the customs and institutions of schools, academies, colleges . . , everything is found adverse to the progress of science, For the lectures and exercises there are so ordered that to think or speculate on anything out of the common way can hardly occur. And if one or two have the boldness to use any liberty of judgment, they must undertake the task all by themselves; they can have no advantage from the company of others."*

**MEDICAL SCIENCE:** Medical science has generally worked hard to retain good relations with religion. Immunology, surgery, and internal medicine, despite the fact they successfully conquered illness and plagues that religious prayer was unable to conquer, doctors in these specialties still show great respect for religion and religious leaders, and go to great lengths to publicly state that spirituality can be as important to a person's health as modern medicine.

And religion responded positively. Hospitals and universities, largely supported by religious organizations, opened their doors to immunology, surgery, and internal medicine, accepting a duality where religion takes care of the spiritual and emotional part of illness, and these medical sciences take care of the physical part.

**But genetics has not faired** too well. The religious monk Mendel, using the scientific method, discovered that man could manipulate genetics, and his work was accepted by religion supported universities. And, later, when Darwin and Wallace discovered that genes could be manipulated by environmental conditions, even this work was accepted though it conflicted with the biblical writers that held that God made the world and the animals in six days.

But then, tactlessly, Darwin published his *Descent of Man,* arguing that man descended from the monkey, when biblical writers had made it clear that man was made in the image of God. It was not only tactless, it was *unscientific*, for science is not interested *where* things come from, and the argument caused such friction between genetics and religion that it spilled over into politics, and has interfered with important stem cell research.

**POLITICAL SCIENCE:** As we are all aware, political science took Bacon's advice to heart. The first act of Congress was to amend the Constitution with a Bill of Rights, and one amendment insured the separation of church and state, and the freedom of religion. And religions have generally responded to the duality positively. Unfortunately, in some parts of the world this duality is not practiced, and those nations have suffered constant conflict and regression.

And this public display of deference to religion was very important to the success of the American political experiment; for, without the aid of The King of France, who held his position by "divine right" in the old ecclesiastical political system, the American Revolution might have been lost. Louis, of course, had political motives, but if the Americans hadn't shown respect for religion, the French king would never have supported them.

I'd like to mention that Bacon would be disappointed at America's current attempt to push our political system on foreign nations by force. He would urge us to let political science improve American politics to demonstrate its success, and allow other nations to decide if they wish to adopt it. Bacon would say that political science, of all the sciences, should never become "dogmatic and magisterial."

*But sciences should be like mines, where the noise of new works and further advances is heard on every side."*

**SO, IF ECONOSCIENTISTS** study the history of science since 1620, they'll discover that science has had its greatest success when it presents itself as a "handmaiden" to religion, and progress is impeded when it becomes dogmatic and magisterial. This is a lesson that advocates of econoscience need to keep in mind; for they will face the largest, most powerful, most durable, and most well-organized idolatry in man's history – the worship of Mammon.

And it is a pagan idolatry with no concept of justice, compassion, mercy or forgiveness to soften its effect. Its most devout worshippers are so brutal that they even despise the poor, the sick, and the unemployed because these poor souls are burdens to the monetary system. And, naturally, they react violently to any attempt to tamper with or threaten the monetary system.

Bacon would say it has been too long, thousands of years that metaphysicians have dominated the study of economics. He'd warn over and over that nature is far more subtle than man's logic. He'd say it is time to set aside all of our well-worn generalities and seek a system of economics that nature intended for man's prosperity, for it is only a natural system that will grow and prosper with use.

And Bacon and Locke would tell econoscientists to remember they are scientists, not crusaders for social change. Their job is to patiently discover every possible *natural* economic system or variation that exists or existed in human behavior before the adoption of the monetary system, test them to determine if they can be developed with modern technology, and then report all details so society can choose whether to incorporate them or not. In short, econoscience is to act as the investigative arm of society, and not as its jury.

And they'd all say econoscientists need for a time to push aside the logical conclusions of metaphysicians like Adam Smith, Karl Marx, and Lenin, and look at the facts as they actually exist in nature, for man's logic is no match for the subtlety of nature. And they would warn that the more certain an idea seems fixed in current logic, such as money is "the grease" of the economy, the more suspect the idea should be held and questioned.

*"The subtlety of nature is greater many times over than the subtlety of man's senses and understanding, so that all those specious meditations, speculations and glosses in which men indulge are quite from the purpose, only there is no one by to observe it."*

*"There is a great difference between the Idols of the human mind and the Ideas of the divine. That is to say, between the empty dogmas, and the true signatures and marks set upon the works of creation as they are found in nature."*

*"And generally let every student of nature take this as a rule – that whatever his mind seizes and dwells upon with peculiar satisfaction is to be held in suspicion, and that so much the more care is to be taken in dealing with such questions to keep the understanding even and clear."*

*"For I am building in the human understanding a true model of the world, such as it is in fact, not such as a man's own reason would have it to be, a thing which cannot be done without a very diligent dissection and anatomy of the world."*

In short, the important thing all would argue is that society needs to establish a special econoscience similar to political science. The new science may very well conclude the monetary system, with some adjustment, is the best of all possible worlds, or that the more natural system suggested by Locke is the best. But, just as often, the new science might also discover in nature a revolutionary new organization that, when developed, will change the course of civilization.

**FORTUNATELY,** there are many reasons for hope of success despite the opposition, for other religions recognize the worship of Mammon is the source of evil, and most are dedicated to taking care of the poor and the sick. These religions, if econoscientists use the tact of Newton and Einstein, may very well support the development of an unbiased econoscience. In fact there's a good chance the major spiritual religions may even become strong advocates of econoscience.

And, too, even the devout worshippers of Mammon are realists. They will support anyone and anything that promises them a profit, and, fortunately, econoscience can do so. As stated, it can honestly promise to work to create a system to allow the poor and unemployed to become self sufficient so they are not a burden on the monetary system. And, furthermore, since the new system will have no need for money, it will never call for any taxes.

And, too, the formation of a commonwealth will only apply to the production side of the economy. The consumer side could remain on the monetary system and unhampered, and that's where the profit lies. So there are in fact many advantages econoscience could offer that could cause supporters of the monetary system to support its development, and even support the institution of economic democracy on the production side of the economy.

Finally, Bacon and Locke and Newton would advise advocates of econoscience to always report honestly, giving the pros and cons of any new system, and to keep a low personal profile. Do this, they'd say, and econoscience will eventually become socially acceptable like physics, medicine and political science, and be able to peacefully nudge vital parts of economic behavior into the Age of Science while we still have the fading twilight of the monetary system.

End